Zoo Animals

Hippopotamus

Patricia Whitehouse

Heinemann Library
Chicago, Illinois

Customer Service 888-454-2279
Visit our website at www.heinemannlibrary.com

Designed by Sue Emerson, Heinemann Library
Printed and bound in the United States by Lake Book Manufacturing, Inc.

07 06 05 04 03
10 9 8 7 6 5 4 3 2 1

Library of Congress Cataloging-in-Publication Data
Whitehouse, Patricia, 1958-
     Hippopotamus / Patricia Whitehouse.
          p. cm. — (Zoo animals)
Includes index.
Summary: An introduction to hippos, including their size, diet and everyday life style, which
highlights differences between those in the wild and those living in a zoo habitat.
     ISBN: 1-58810-899-6 (HC), 1-40340-645-6 (Pbk.)
     1. Hippopotamidae—Juvenile literature. [1. Hippopotamus. 2. Zoo animals.] I. Title.
QL737.U57 W55 2002
599.63'5—dc21
                    2001007442

Acknowledgments
The author and publishers are grateful to the following for permission to reproduce copyright material:
Title page, p. 11 James P. Rowan/DRK Photo; pp. 4, 20 M. Harvey/DRK Photo; p. 5 Morton Beebe/Corbis; pp. 6, 22, 24 Chicago Zoological Society/The Brookfield Zoo; p. 7T Tom & Pat Leeson/DRK Photo; p. 7B Erwin & Peggy Bauer/Bruce Coleman Inc.; p. 8 Joe McDonald/Visuals Unlimited; p. 9 Stephen J. Krasemann/DRK Photo; p. 10 Wolfgang Kaehler/ Corbis; p. 12 Kennan Ward/Corbis; p. 13 Jo Prater/Visuals Unlimited; p. 14 G. L. E./Visuals Unlimited; p. 15 Peter & Beverly Pickford/Visuals Unlimited; p. 16 ABPL/M. Harvey/Animals Animals/Earth Science; p. 17 OSF/Alan Root/Animals Animals/Earth Science; p. 18 Barbara Cushman Rowell/DRK Photos; p. 19 Darrell Gulin/DRK Photo; p. 21T Chicago Zoological Society/The Brookfield Zoo; p. 21B Tom Brakefield/Corbis; p. 23 (T-B) Joe McDonald/ Visuals Unlimited, Chicago Zoological Society/The Brookfield Zoo, Jim Schulz/Chicago Zoological Society/The Brookfield Zoo/Heinemann Library, Corbis; back cover (L-R) Morton Beebe/Corbis, Chicago Zoological Society/The Brookfield Zoo

Cover photograph by Chicago Zoological Society/The Brookfield Zoo
Photo research by Bill Broyles

Every effort has been made to contact copyright holders of any material reproduced in this book. Any omissions will be rectified in subsequent printings if notice is given to the publisher.

Special thanks to our advisory panel for their help in the preparation of this book:

Eileen Day, Preschool Teacher
Chicago, IL

Ellen Dolmetsch,
Library Media Specialist
Wilmington, DE

Kathleen Gilbert,
Teacher
Round Rock, TX

Sandra Gilbert,
Library Media Specialist
Houston, TX

Angela Leeper,
Educational Consultant
North Carolina Department
of Public Instruction
Raleigh, NC

Pam McDonald, Reading Teacher
Winter Springs, FL

Melinda Murphy,
Library Media Specialist
Houston, TX

We would also like to thank Lee Haines, Assistant Director of Marketing and Public Relations at the Brookfield Zoo in Brookfield, Illinois, for his review of this book.

Some words are shown in bold, **like this.**
You can find them in the picture glossary on page 23.

Contents

What Are Hippopotamuses?

Hippopotamuses are **mammals.**

Mammals have hair or fur on their bodies.

People call hippopotamuses "hippos."

You can see hippos at the zoo.

What Do Hippos Look Like?

Hippos have big bodies and short legs.

Their skin is mostly dark gray.

Most hippos are as big as a car.

Some hippos are only as big
as a table.

What Do Baby Hippos Look Like?

A baby hippo looks like its parents, but it is smaller.

A baby hippo is called a **calf**.

New calves are mostly pink.

They turn gray as they get older.

Where Do Hippos Live?

In the wild, hippos live in rivers and lakes.

They live where it is warm all year.

At the zoo, hippos live in **enclosures.**

The enclosures have pools of water.

What Do Hippos Eat?

In the wild, hippos eat grass.

They tear the grass with their strong lips.

At the zoo, hippos eat grass and **hay**.

They also eat apples and carrots.

What Do Hippos Do All Day?

Hippos spend the day sleeping.

They sleep in the water or on land.

Hippos can be mostly underwater and still breathe.

They float so that the tops of their heads stick out.

What Do Hippos Do at Night?

Hippos wake up at night to eat.

They leave the water to find grass.

They also walk along the bottom of rivers.

They eat plants that grow underwater.

What Sounds Do Hippos Make?

Hippos make grunting sounds.

They are loud enough to be heard far away.

Hippos also grunt to each other underwater.

How Are Hippos Special?

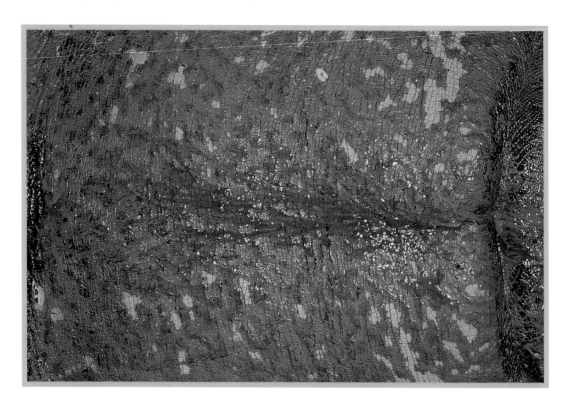

Hippos can get sunburned.

They have a red oil on their skin to keep it safe from the sun.

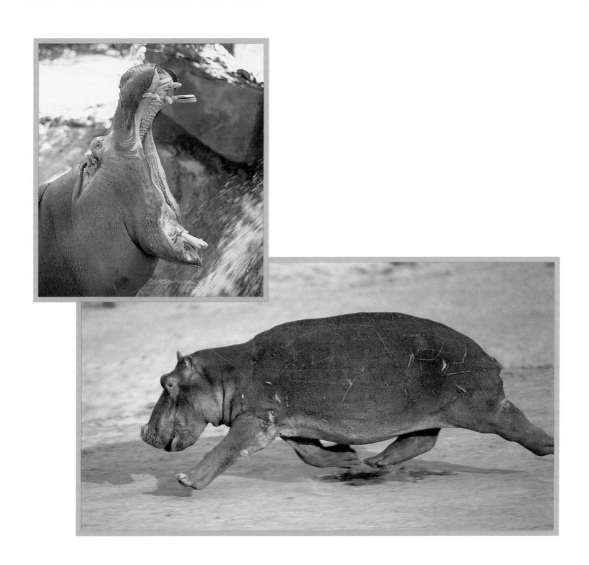

Hippos can open their mouths very wide.

They can run fast on land.

Quiz

Do you remember what these hippo parts are called?

Look for the answers on page 24.

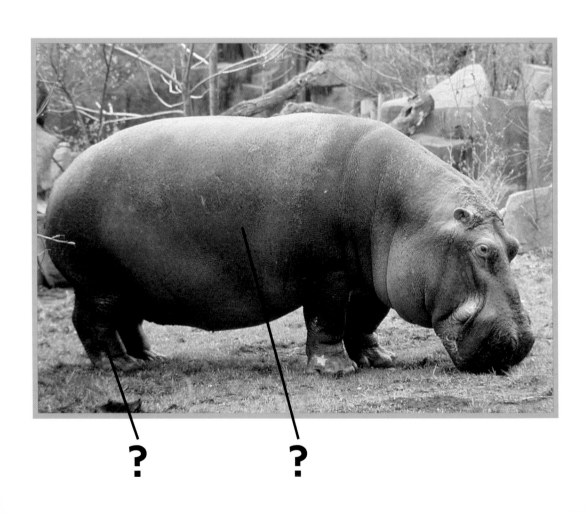

?   ?

Picture Glossary

 **calf**
pages 8, 9

 **enclosure**
page 11

 **hay**
page 13

 **mammal**
page 4

Note to Parents and Teachers

Reading for information is an important part of a child's literacy development. Learning begins with a question about something. Help children think of themselves as investigators and researchers by encouraging their questions about the world around them. In this book, the animal is identified as a mammal. A mammal is an animal that is covered with hair or fur and that feeds its young with milk from its body. The symbol for mammal in the picture glossary is a dog nursing its babies. Point out that although the photograph for mammal shows a dog, many other animals are mammals—including humans.

Index

Answers to quiz on page 22

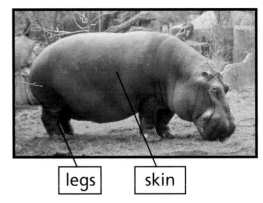

legs   skin

24